23

A Country Preacher,
His Grandson,
And A Devotional That
Will Change Your Life.

Mitchel Whitington

ISBN
0-9801850-0-9 (10 digit)
978-0-9801850-0-3 (13 digit)

Library of Congress Control Number: 2007939901

Second Edition

Printed in the United States of America
Published by 23 House Publishing
SAN 299-8084
www.23house.com

For Granddad, the country preacher
who wrote this book with me...

Table of Contents

Chapter 1: The 23rd Psalm

What an incredible journey this book has been. It all started over a year ago, at a low time in my life, when I was desperately looking for direction. I was a partner in a company that was crippled by a series of disastrous events. I had health issues that were terrifying me, and I was seriously considering giving up a career that I loved and had worked extremely hard to build. Those were dark, dark days.

One morning a book that my grandfather had written some thirty-odd years ago caught my eye. For years the book had been displayed next to Granddad's picture on a table that I passed by many times a day. On that particular occasion, I was suddenly and inexplicably drawn to it. As I sat down and read Granddad's book, the words of that wonderful, old country preacher taught me the meaning of the 23rd Psalm.

I'd memorized it in Sunday School as a boy, and still pretty much knew it by word by word, but I had never really thought about the individual verses that comprised it and what they were actually saying. I could tell you that my heart was touched that day, but that's not an adequate description – it was much more powerful than that. It was almost as if the skies opened up and God reached down and embraced me.

Through months of contemplation and meditation on the 23rd Psalm, I saw God's power change my life. I realized that I wasn't meant to lead some mediocre existence, plodding through my days and simply getting by. God wanted more for me, but it wasn't He that was lacking... it was me, and the words of the 23rd Psalm helped show me the way back.

My life changed radically in ways that I never could have imagined. I found myself wanting to share this with everyone that I met. My first thought was that I needed to get Granddad's book out onto the shelves where people could read it; the manuscript had never been traditionally published, since it was something that he had done only for friends, family and congregation.

As inspiring as his words were, though, they needed some tweaking. For example, he noted that one of the greatest threats to the countries of the world was that of Communism – a very real sentiment in the 1970s, but our post-9/11 world has changed a bit. The fact that some country might become Communist is nothing compared to the very real concern that a terrorist could set off a nuclear bomb in the heart of any American city. As I went through it, though, I couldn't help but smile; although some of the details needed to be updated, the message was timeless.

I started with his book on the 23rd Psalm as a basis, and added some contemporary examples that would be more appropriate to today's reader. I first separated my words from his, but it turned out to be an awkward read; it was full of "Granddad said this" and "I'm saying that" ...well, you get the idea.

I struggled with how to proceed, and tried many different ways to organize the book, none of which seemed to flow any better. Maintaining the essence of Granddad's thoughts about the 23rd Psalm was paramount, but making it easy and enjoyable to read was also important; the Psalm has a message that must be told. In the end, I combined our words and voices together as one, and added several anecdotes about my Grandfather from my point of view, because his life keenly illustrates the journey – and the blessings – spelled out in the 23rd Psalm.

To put this book together, I drew not only from his original text, but also from a collection of his sermons that I am fortunate to have. Most Biblical references come from Granddad, because no one knew the Good Book like him. I remember that he was preaching one Sunday morning, and during the scripture reading, there was some snickering out in the congregation. Granddad couldn't figure out why, because the topic was very serious. After the sermon, some of the members informed him that as he was reading from the Bible, he was holding it upside down. He knew the scripture that well – there are some people who are convinced to this day that he had the entire Bible committed to memory.

By the way, all the scriptural references are from the King James Version of the Bible, but I encourage you to read them in your favorite translation. Granddad loved the King James Version, so I'm sticking with it in this book to honor him.

My grandfather died over twenty years ago on August 21, 1987. That's not the end of his story, though; he left behind children, grandchildren, great-grandchildren and members of his congregation that will always remember "Brother Kirk." He touched many, many lives, and through these words on the 23rd Psalm, I am confident that he will touch many more.

It is an honor and a pleasure to write this book with him; at times, I could swear that I felt him looking over my shoulder.

I worked on this book carefully and prayerfully, because anytime that someone gives observations about the scripture, they are accountable to God. In Revelation 22, John cautions about commenting on the Bible; he says that if any man adds to the words in the book, God's going to give him the plagues described in the Bible, and if any man takes away from the words in the book, God takes away his name from Heaven and everything there. That's an extremely strong statement, and one that I am very mindful of. The Old Testament says much the same thing in Deuteronomy 4:2: *You shall not add to the word which I command you, nor take from it, that you may keep the commandments of the Lord your God.*

To be honest, I'm really not nervous about answering to God about this book; I feel satisfied that I've stayed faithful to my Grandfather's convictions regarding the 23rd Psalm, and I know from personal experience how powerful that passage of

3

scripture is. I am aware, however, that when it comes my time to leave this life, I'll meet up with Granddad again, and I think that I'm just a tad nervous about that.

You see, my Grandmother died several years after he did, and before she passed away, she was lying in the hospital bed chattering away to him, just as if he was standing right there in the room. I feel certain he was – that he'd come to comfort her during her last hours on Earth. I can only imagine that he was telling her about the glories of God and the magnificence of Heaven. As I am lying on my deathbed, though, I think that Granddad might come to see me, and from the moment that I first spot him, he'll probably be asking questions about this book. "Why in the world did you tell that story about me?" or "Didn't you check my notes on that particular verse? I wanted to add some supporting scripture!"

If I really stop to think and about it, though, I feel sure that he'll be happy with it. There've been too many interesting coincidences in the course of writing this book, and to be honest, I don't believe in coincidences at all. I'm convinced that he's been a part of the project from the very start.

Granddad loved the 23rd Psalm. In fact, he always said that it is the heart of the Bible, because it deals directly with the basic issues in the human experience. It speaks to each of us personally, and is perhaps the most fundamental, awesome and systematic discussion of God's plan for dealing with each of us as individuals.

Out of all the adjectives that can be used to describe the 23rd Psalm, the one that I like most is *profound*. That distills it down to its very essence. I firmly believe – and I know for a fact – that if you study the passage, meditate on it, and believe it in your heart, your life will change in ways that you can't even begin to comprehend right now. God's plan for the direction for your life is spelled out *exactly* in the words of the 23rd Psalm.

It's a short little chapter of the Bible; there are only six verses and 118 words in the King James Version of the Psalm, and seventeen of them are pronouns in the first person. It is that *personal* element that makes the Psalm so incomparably sweet and appealing in its message – it finds an echo in the heart of all humanity.

This is how the Psalmist describes the relationship that God desires to have with you:

Psalm 23

[1]*The Lord is my shepherd; I shall not want.*

[2]*He maketh me to lie down in green pastures: he leadeth me beside the still waters.*

[3]*He restoreth my soul: he leadeth me in the paths of righteousness for his name's sake.*

[4]*Yea, though I walk through the valley of the shadow of death, I will fear no evil: for thou art with me; thy rod and thy staff they comfort me.*

[5]*Thou preparest a table before me in the presence of mine enemies: thou anointest my head with oil; my cup runneth over.*

[6]*Surely goodness and mercy shall follow me all the days of my life: and I will dwell in the house of the Lord for ever.*

These simple verses each hold God's infinite promises and power, and they are there waiting for you to discover. It's easy to read those words and skip through their familiar refrains, but this book is about getting more out of them. It's about discovering the power in the promises that God has placed in the 23rd Psalm, and finding out how it can enrich your life.

To do this, take Granddad's advice and study the 23rd Psalm carefully; come with me as we take this incredible chapter of the Bible verse by verse, and spend time examining each one to find out how it applies to our lives.

Before we start looking at the Psalm, let me say one final thing: this book is only a springboard to the new life that awaits you. I believe that if you start down the road of studying the 23rd Psalm, you will find truths specific to your own life and needs that far exceed any expectations that you may have now.

Finally, here are a few words from that old, country preacher himself, Brother Kirk:

"The 23rd Psalm is intriguing. I have been intrigued by it all my Christian life and will be even in eternity. The Psalmist says in Psalm 119:89: *Forever O Lord, thy word is settled in heaven.* And the prophet Isaiah in chapter 40, verse 8, expresses it this way: *The grass withereth, the flower fadeth; but the word of our God shall stand for ever.* Jesus said in Matthew 24:35: *Heaven and earth shall pass away, but my words shall not pass away.* Yes, in Heaven God's word will still intrigue me."

I would dare to say that the 23rd Psalm is still one of Granddad's favorite verses of scripture, just as it is mine. As you explore its powerful message, I feel certain that it will become one of yours as well.

Chapter 2: The Lord Is My Shepherd

The Lord is my shepherd; I shall not want. This is an infinitely powerful opening to the Psalm, yet is something that we typically tend to recite without thought or emotion. I'm glad that the 23rd Psalm doesn't begin with a prayer begging God for something. It merely states a fact: the Lord is my shepherd, and I shall not want. That simple, yet mighty beginning to the Psalm spells out God's attitude toward His people, and the specific relationship that He wants to have with you as an individual.

The Psalmist must have chosen this metaphor because it could be so easily understood at the time of its writing – shepherding was a very common profession in those days. A shepherd had to be extremely familiar with his flock, so that at a glance he would know if one had wandered off. A shepherd also had to lead the flock to pastures where grass was plentiful so that they would not go hungry, and where there was water that was safe to drink. In addition, the shepherd had to be ready at any time to protect his flock from predators seeking to do them harm. It was a profession with many responsibilities – of total and complete responsibility, in fact.

I shall not want – consider the fact that want is not desire, but need. Actually, it's the sum total of all material, mental, moral and spiritual needs. But be careful to understand the difference between desire and need. If you were to stand up and declare, "I want to walk on the moon!" does that mean that God is going to make that happen? Probably not. We live in an age where there hasn't been moon travel for years; if anyone were to walk on the moon again in our lifetime, it would be an astronaut with flight experience and training. Furthermore, even though God's power is infinite and he could place you on the moon by the time that you draw your next breath, what would it serve? Asking God for such an outlandish thing would be ridiculous. You might desire a time machine to travel back and see the dinosaurs, or you could have a strong desire to be king of the entire world. Those aren't things that you *need* for your life, however.

In the Old Testament, Joshua called upon God to make the sun and moon stand still in the sky so that he could complete the battle in which his people were engaged – and it was done! Think about the awesome power that it would take to accomplish such a celestial feat... but that was nothing for God, who created the stars and the planets with his own hands. He granted Joshua's request, and literally stopped the sun and the moon for a day. I wonder what would happen if you called on God to do the same thing? Do you think that He would do that for you? There's no question that He *could*, of course, with the same ease that He did for Joshua... but what would that accomplish? Even if you were to ask Him for that miracle, it's not something that you need.

On the other hand, there are many blessings that you could use: a good education for your children, healing for yourself or a friend, a job that you look forward to every day, a loving family surrounding you, or financial security for the future. Any of those things could be put to practical application, to make your life more rich and productive. These are things that you need on this Earth for a better life, and the kinds of blessings that God has waiting for you. Paul put it this way in Romans 8:32: *He that spared not his own Son, but delivered him up for us all; how shall he not with him also freely give us all things?*

The Bible is full of examples of what God wants for you. In Philippians 4:19, Paul says: *But my God shall supply all your needs according to his riches in glory by Christ Jesus.*

And the Psalmist says in Psalm 84:11: *The Lord will give grace and glory; no good thing will he withhold from them that walk uprightly.*

Finally, John 16:23-24 states, *Whatsoever ye shall ask the Father in my name, he will give it to you.*

Those verses are just a sampling of the abundance that God wants to bless you with. It doesn't say, "He wants to give you enough to scrape by," or "He'll provide just what you need to survive." Just the opposite, in fact. Isaiah 1:19 says: *If ye be willing and obedient, ye shall eat the good of the land.*

The good of the land – the bounty! Go back and re-read those verses: He will freely give you all things; He shall supply your needs; no good thing will He withhold from you. Whatever you ask for in His name, you will receive. How much clearer does He have to say it? God desires to provide for you as totally and completely as a shepherd does for his sheep.

My grandfather expected and received the blessings that God had for him throughout his life – even the little things. You see, Granddad loved to fish. He used lures instead of live bait, because as he once told me, "I'm not patient enough to wait for the fish to come to me; I've got to take it to them."

On a preacher's salary, however, he didn't have the luxury of running to the sporting goods store and buying all the latest tackle and lures. No, he made his own. He'd taken several squares of plaster, a little smaller and a bit thicker than a slice of bread, and carved out the shape of half a fishing jig in each one. When the squares were fitted together, they formed a mold for the complete lure, with a groove to position the hook in, and a hole in the mold in which to pour the lead. When it came time to make new lures, he'd fit the mold halves together, and bind them with rubber bands. Fishhooks would have already been positioned inside in those little tracks carved out to exactly fit them. He and my grandmother would melt the lead in a pan on the stove, and then working together, they would pour the liquid metal into the molds. After it cooled, he opened the molds and used his knife to trim up the lures. Finally, he'd dress it up with paint, feathers and pipe cleaners.

Those homemade jigs worked incredibly well. One day he was fishing at the local lake and having quite a bit of success. A man approached him and asked how many he'd caught. My grandfather told him, and the man said, "Well, I'm a Game Warden; are you aware that's your legal limit?" Now, Granddad was always a stickler for obeying the law, but since he was talking to an official who controlled such things, without missing a beat he smiled and said, "Tell you what... give me your permission to catch just one more fish, and I'll give you the jig that I'm using." The Game Warden thought about it for a second, then nodded his head and said, "Deal!" Granddad landed a final bass, and then took his fish home to clean them. The Game Warden stuck the lure in his pocket and probably looked forward to taking off work a little early that day.

Of course, the only problem with making the jigs was the lead – fishing hooks were cheap, and he collected scrap feathers, pipe cleaners and the other adornments to use. On a preacher's salary, every penny counted, and you certainly couldn't characterize fishing as a necessity. Having some fish to fry up for dinner helped out, but they were by no means going to starve without them. It wasn't a requirement for his life. Still, my Granddad loved to fish.

I remember one day when I was spending the afternoon with them and a member of his congregation came by to visit. They talked about the church, the Bible, the news, and a couple of problems that the man was having. As always, at the close of a personal visit Granddad prayed, and then walked the gentleman outside. I distinctly remember the man saying, "By the way, Brother Kirk, I've got something for you." He went around to the trunk of his car and hefted out a big block of lead. "I know that you make your own fishing lures, so let's cut you off a chunk." He put the block on the concrete front porch, produced a knife that looked huge to a young boy like me, and sliced off a piece of lead that was a couple of inches thick. I

10

marveled at how easily the blade seemed to go through the soft metal. Granddad thanked him, and we went back inside.

It wasn't long until a chunk of the lead was in a pan on the stove, about to be turned into one of the world's best fishing jigs. Because the Lord was his shepherd, Granddad did not want – not even for lead to make fishing lures.

I love declaring this first sentence of the 23rd Psalm out loud throughout the day: *The Lord is my shepherd; I shall not want!* Whether I'm in the shower getting ready to start the day, in the car driving along a highway, or even walking down the street, there is a confidence that I get from saying those words aloud. People who read the 23rd Psalm often just pass over that incredible opening, that mighty declaration of faith, and it is unfortunate that they do. I love saying them, and there are times when I've stood in my house and shouted the words at the top of my lungs: "THE LORD IS MY SHEPHERD; I *SHALL NOT WANT.*"

The words are that powerful, and that important. Stop and think about them – with the Lord as your shepherd, you *will never want!*

Chapter 3: In Green Pastures

He maketh me to lie down in green pastures. Many words have been written about this verse throughout the years, most concerning the idyllic image of lush, green fields stretching out as far as the eye can see. The visual is incredible – you can easily imagine lying down in a pasture of soft, green grass on a lazy spring afternoon. From the shepherd's point of view, it is an even more important image. He has provided his sheep a soft place to rest: a grassy pasture, instead of a rocky, scraggly hillside. This is also a place where the sheep can graze. Not only can they eat their fill, but they can then take a nap on a perfect bed. This verse always reminds me of Thanksgiving; my wife cooks the turkey overnight, so we wake up in the morning smelling the delightful scent. It's a little bit of aromatic heaven all day until we finally sit down to a delicious, bountiful meal, where I am all but certain to be guilty of the sin of gluttony. As soon as the meal is over and we've done the dishes, I find my way to the couch for a nap, and it may be the best sleep that I experience all year long. I am truly lying down in green pastures.

That image alone made it one of my favorite verses in the 23rd Psalm – before I really started studying it, that is. Once I read Granddad's book and began meditating on the individual scriptures, this particular one terrified me.

My first impulse was to deny it – to focus back on the first verse of the Psalm alone. But to truly accept the blessings that God has in store for you, it is important to understand and embrace all aspects of the relationship that is spelled out in the 23rd Psalm. You see, this second verse says that He not only provides the green pastures, but He *maketh* me lie down in them. There is something compulsory and definitive about the word maketh – note that the Psalmist doesn't say that the Lord might *suggest* that I lie down, and He doesn't *recommend* that I lie down, nor does it say that the pasture is there should I *choose* to lie down… He *makes* me lie down. When He makes us lie down, sometimes it's hard to see the green pastures; but that doesn't mean that they aren't there.

When talking about this verse, Granddad said, "I read somewhere that great poems were not written on busy streets, and lovely songs were not composed in the midst of great crowds. Our vision of God comes when we are stopped. Even Jesus withdrew from the multitudes and went into the mountains to commune with the Father."

The Bible says, *Be still and know that I am God* (Psalm 46:10). It's that "being still" that is hard for us; our lives are hectic, and if you're like me, it is sometimes overwhelming. We're busy with jobs, relationships, activities, children, hobbies, movies, sports, television… well, the list goes on forever. It's no wonder that sometimes God has to slow us down to hear His voice and to do His will. It may be in some way that initially seems like a catastrophe – losing a job, becoming ill, hitting financial straits, or falling prey to any of life's pitfalls. That can be God's hand making us lie down, however, for a purpose that is greater than we can imagine at the time.

The Bible is full of instances when the Lord made someone lie down – to slow up, take time off, or simply just change their present situation. Even though not apparent at the time, the purpose was crucial, and the final reward great. For example, the Lord made Paul to lie down by putting him in prison, but while he was there he wrote the Biblical books of Galatians, Ephesians, Philippians, Colossians and II Timothy. David was sold into slavery, but the situation worked to escalate him to be the high office of King – one of the greatest that the world has ever known. It's easy to recite this verse, *He maketh me to lie down in green pastures*, but imagine if that meant that you were to find yourself imprisoned, or even more unthinkable, sold into slavery… and that was the way that God made you to lie down.

That part blows my mind; it's much more natural to say, Lord, give me your blessings, but I don't want anything bad to happen to me! The walk with God that is described in the 23rd Psalm is a journey of faith, however, and you have to be confident that when you are made to lie down, there will be green pastures there waiting for you. Here's what my Grandfather said about the subject over thirty years ago:

"The Lord made many preachers to preach, even me. *He maketh me to lie down* – I have thought about this statement lately. After eighty years of life I had a blood clot in my left leg. A year later I had to have prostate gland surgery. The year that I'm writing this I had a heart attack on January 14th, and on May 24th I had a stroke. He maketh me to lie down. I am unable to preach at this time. I am writing these words on the 23rd Psalm in order to keep proclaiming that the Good Shepherd gave His life for His sheep. Sometimes God makes us to lie down in rest, or sorrow, sometimes in sickness, sometimes in afflictions. We are told in II Corinthians 4:17: *For our light affliction, which is but for a moment, worketh for a far more exceeding and eternal weight of glory.* II Corinthians 12:9-10 comforts such times with the words: *And he said unto me, My grace is sufficient for thee: for my strength is made perfect in weakness. Most gladly therefore will I rather glory in my infirmities, that the power of Christ may rest upon me. Therefore I take pleasure in infirmities, in reproaches, in necessities, in persecutions, in distresses for Christ's sake: for when I am weak, then am I strong.* I am confident that my health problems, although they have slowed me down, are being used for the greater glory of God!"

After all of his illnesses, it's hard to imagine my Grandfather still celebrating his life. I feel certain that if I were him, I'd be tempted toward anger – to become frustrated and say, "Lord, I've made a life of the ministry and trying to serve you... is this how you reward me as I come into my golden years?"

Not Granddad, though. I think that he realized that the Lord had slowed him down for a purpose: to write down his comments and convictions on the 23rd Psalm. After all, if he was still able to preach, he might never have found the time. If he had kept forging actively ahead through life until his dying day, writing a book about his favorite scripture might never have happened. It apparently was something that he was supposed to accomplish, but to get it done, the Lord had to make him slow down a bit.

He wrote it sitting at their dining room table, pecking it out on a typewriter, enjoying his life with my Grandmother. He was greatly limited in his physical activities but he still could sit in his favorite chair and watch the news every day. He ate Grandmother's delicious home cooking and there was a never-ending parade of members of the various churches where he had preached and served. Maybe his biggest contribution in this season of his life was his ability to record his words about a lifetime of meditation on the 23rd Psalm to share with his family, his friends, with his grandson, and now with you. When God made him lie down, it truly was in green pastures.

Of course, when you are made to lie down, it's not always a dramatic event; sometimes it's quite subtle. For example, my wife and I were out of town for the weekend a while back and we had an extremely full schedule. Because of that, we didn't take anything for work or leisure – no books, no laptop, no DVDs, no briefcase, nothing. When we reached our destination on Friday, we checked into our hotel and started the whirlwind of weekend activities. About 6 PM, the event that we were attending began to break up and we found out that some plans had been cancelled, miscommunications had occurred, and we basically had twenty-four hours of downtime until our next event. We walked out to the parking lot a little dumbfounded; we were in a town we weren't familiar with, with absolutely no agenda or work resources. As we drove away, we lamented the fact that so much time was going to be wasted; if we'd only known and prepared, we could have gotten a tremendous amount of work done. Instead we had nothing to do but return to the hotel and sit... which is exactly what we did. In fact, we put on our pajamas, propped up on the pillows and pulled up the covers, then proceeded to watch old movies on television for hours. We talked and laughed until we finally fell asleep – and then in the morning, picked right back up with another show. We spent a couple of hours of just sipping coffee and relaxing. We talked, we reminisced, we reflected on how crazy life tends to get. By the time that our next commitment rolled around, we'd decided that it was one of the best weekends in a long, long time. It would have been so easy to stress out over the loss of productive hours and just gripe and fret all weekend, but it turned out much better to simply say, "Okay, we've been made to lie down, there must be a reason." Looking back, the reason was obviously that we needed a break and some simple together-time that we might not otherwise have taken – and our lives are all the richer for it.

It is extremely easy for us to question God's will in times of inconvenience or adversity. In the past, you may have wondered, "Why did I get laid off from that job that I loved?" or "Why am I so sick?" On the weekend that I just talked about, we initially couldn't understand why the hectic schedule had cleared so quickly and completely, and left us unprepared. There is a purpose for everything, though. The Lord might be making you lie down, but that's only half of it – the place that He's provided for you is a lush, green pasture. Instead of complaining about what is causing you to "lie down," look for the green pasture in your life. You might be amazed at what you find.

Chapter 4: Beside The Still Waters

He leadeth me beside the still waters. The folks who are familiar with shepherding say that sheep are afraid of running water; they are much more at ease drinking from a tranquil pool. A shepherd would have known every possible source of water in the surrounding area where he was grazing his sheep, and would lead them to a place of peaceful water where they could drink and not be afraid.

By leading his sheep to still water, the shepherd is dealing with their fear, which is what this verse is all about – just like the shepherd, God does not want you to fear or be afraid.

The Bible says: *Let not your heart be troubled, neither let it be afraid* (John 14:27)... but it's just not that easy. As humans, we fear many, many things – it is our nature.

I know that my Granddad had his hands full helping Grandmother stay "beside the still waters." Besides being an excellent cook and homemaker, she was a world-class worrier – I think that she feared everything. The stories about her in our family indicate that she could find some reason to be afraid in almost every situation, but Granddad had learned to live beside the still waters and he knew how to comfort her. His favorite phrase was "Honey, it'll be all right." He knew that the Lord was their Shepherd and no problem that they faced was too overwhelming for Him.

Granddad was good at comforting fears, and I think that's why he loved to use examples when he talked about this verse. There's no way to cover every possible fear that we might face, but here are just a few of the things that confront us on a daily basis...

Fear of the past. It is easy to dwell on bad decisions that we have made, unfortunate things that have happened to us,

19

and hurts that we have suffered or hurts we have caused. Who hasn't looked back at something in their life and said, "If only I hadn't done that!" Thankfully, even with all the bad decisions that we may have made, or people that we have wronged, or sins that we have committed, God will forgive us – we have only to ask. God says in Isaiah 43:25 that He blots out your transgressions, and will not remember your sins. Do you understand what that verse is saying? He is going to forgive you and will not even *remember* your sins. How awesome is that! There is nothing in your past that is so bad that God won't forgive you, and then *forget that it ever happened.* That's an incredible promise that He makes.

Fear of the future. I've heard it said that the source of our greatest worry is tomorrow. We worry about the state of our jobs, our health, our finances, and our relationships. Believe me, I find myself falling prey to such worries all the time. When I do, though, I look to these words of wisdom from Granddad: "Don't worry about the future, because God sees it with the clarity that you see the past. In fact, He is the author of the future. He can be trusted." Consider again the first verse of the 23rd Psalm: *The Lord is my shepherd; I shall not want.* There are no future wants that you may have – none at all – that He cannot fulfill. If you have any worries or doubts, just go back and read that verse again.

Fear of failure. God doesn't want us to fail; in fact, He wants us to flourish in a state of prosperity. In Psalm 1:3 we read that: *And whatsoever he doeth shall prosper.* Not that we won't have setbacks; in fact, several years ago a very good friend of mine experienced what he thought was an insurmountable roadblock. He needed to get his car repaired so that he could get to work every day, and the repair job was going to cost $200 for parts and labor – the only problem was that it was a low time of the month and he literally had under a hundred bucks to his name. He had the brilliant idea of cashing in part of a retirement fund to get some extra money, but when

20

he called the investment company, it turned out to be a very complicated process. There were qualifications and waiting periods, and although the money in the account belonged to him, he couldn't touch it for ninety days – far outside of the boundary of getting his car repaired. In desperation, he was looking for any way to bring money in: donating blood, selling some of his tools, and a yard sale to generate some quick cash. He later told me that on the morning that he was going to start all that, he bowed his head and said, "Lord, I know that I've asked for a lot over the years, but I really, really, really need something special to happen. Please let all these things come together to give me the money that I need." There was no flash of lightning, no clap of thunder, but two interesting things happened within a few hours' time. The first one was that a friend that he hadn't spoken to in months called out of the clear blue and in conversation, found out that my friend was having car troubles; he recommended a garage that could do the same repairs for about half the cost. The second was that in the mail that day was an envelope containing a check for $200, a payment that he was owed for a job that he'd done long ago, and had written off as a loss. Not only did he have the money that he needed, but he suddenly had a surplus to get him through the rest of the month. While he might have felt the pain of failure when he couldn't get ready cash from his investments, in reality that idea stalled because something unexpected – something that would be far beyond his wildest hopes – was already in the works. If you do experience failure, know that it is only part of God's plan because something better for you is about to emerge.

Fear of loneliness. Whether you are willing to admit it or not, this one can be huge. We all worry about being left completely and totally alone. Take heart, though; Hebrews 13:5 says: *I will never leave thee, nor forsake thee.* Loneliness is something that intimidates me, especially as I look toward my later years ahead. My wife and I don't have any kids, so there have been many occasions when I worry about times to come. As friends and family pass away, our circle will continually shrink. Extended family – cousins, nieces and nephews – have dispersed across the country and will probably continue to do so. I fear that there will be a time when it is just my wife and me, alone. After Granddad had written his book on the 23rd Psalm, his health continued to deteriorate, and a second stroke affected his physical body greatly. Caring for him was too big a strain on my grandmother, who had been the healthy one of the pair. Her heart unexpectedly gave out, and she was suddenly in intensive care with a bleak prognosis. The doctors said that if she did actually live, she would never recover and would need to go straight from the hospital to a nursing home. The decision was made, and the arrangements finalized, but my grandmother wanted to be the one to tell Granddad. At the hospital, my parents put her in their car, where he was waiting in the back seat, and they started the drive to the care facility. Mustering all her courage, she blurted out to him, "I've got to go to a nursing home…" Although a stroke had taken his ability to speak clearly, he managed a smile, and gently reached out to pat her hand. After a lifetime together, he wasn't going to let her be alone. He was going to stay with her no matter what – he would never think of leaving her side. That incident in his life to me is a perfect metaphor for God's love; no matter what adversity confronts us, He wants to stand by us – He won't let us face it alone. I don't know what might lie ahead of me in my life, but I do find comfort in the words of Psalm 27:10: *Even if my father and mother abandon me, the Lord will hold me close.* If my family all pass away before I do, if my friends are gone, I know that the Lord will hold me close. I see living examples around me even today, of those people in my life who have lost loved ones but refuse to be alone; they embrace life, they cherish each day, and seem to dare the world to make them feel alone. With such inspiration around me, I do not fear loneliness; the Lord will always be with me.

Fear of old age. Some people have just begun to excel in their later years. For example, Goethe finished *Faust* at the age of 82. Alfred Lord Tennyson wrote his masterful poem "Crossing the Bar" at 80. At the age of 84, William Ewart Gladstone was the Prime Minister of England. General Booth was carrying on the Salvation Army at 86. Antonio Stradivari was making violins at 93, and some of those Stradivarius violins are valued at over a million dollars. Verdi turned out *Ava Maria* at the age of 83. Titian painted the "Battle of Lepanto" at age 98. Justice Oliver Wendell Homes set down some of his most brilliant opinions at aged 90. Michelangelo completed his greatest work at 87, and upon the celebration of his birthday that year observed, "Ancora Imparo," which translates to "I am still learning" (I have a plaque with that engraved on it in my office, by the way). I find comfort in the fact that I have loved every age that I have been. As I rapidly approach fifty, when I am asked what age I would return to if I could pick any point in my life, I've always said, "I'd like to stop right now; this is the best." The odd thing is that I've been saying that since I was in my twenties. But at 25, I didn't know how interesting life would be at 35; and at 35, I had no idea how much fun 45 would be. I fully expect this trend to continue, a fact that I remind myself of whenever I find a fear of aging creeping into my mind. Sure, I could run faster and jump higher thirty years ago, but I have joys now that I could not have imagined back then. Age is only a number. As a teenager, I distinctly remember thinking, "Wow, someday I'm going to be twenty... that's OLD!" In contrast to that, a friend of my father-in-law was turning eighty, and at his birthday party someone asked him what he thought of getting older. He just smiled and said, "Oh, to be seventy again!" Old age has its joys and opportunities – certainly no less than that of youth.

The items in the above paragraphs are only a few of the things that people find to fear – but Granddad used them to show how they can be dealt with. God's plan for our lives has no place for such an emotion as fear. The Psalmist wrote, *he leads us beside the still waters,* and that is the kind of life that God wants you to lead – one that is utterly and completely without fear.

I love my Granddad's take on this verse; he said: "He leadeth me beside still waters... David is not the only man who ever lived that can claim these words. Every child of God can make the same claim. Every believer has the right to claim all the promises of God. I claim the promise that is found in the book of Isaiah 41:10: *Fear thou not; for I am with thee: be not dismayed; for I am thy God: I will strengthen thee; yea, I will help thee; yea, I will uphold thee with the right hand of my righteousness.* This verse in the book of Isaiah has been a triumphant declaration to me in sixty-three years of preaching God's word, and as His child."

The verse that he chose was perfect, for it sums up God's intentions for his people well: fear not – I am with you; don't worry, because I am God; I'll strengthen you; I'll help you; and I'll uphold you. This is how God wants to help you with any fears that you may have in life – these are the still waters that He will lead you beside.

Chapter 5: He Restoreth My Soul

He restoreth my soul. When I was in high school, I made money during the summers by hauling hay. The man that I worked for would spend days on his tractor: cutting the hay, raking it into rows, and then compressing it into rectangular bales. My friends and I would then work as a team to load it onto a trailer for transportation to the barn, where it would be stacked for use during the winter.

Those were wonderful days that I'll always remember, but the work was brutal. I recall coming home in the evening covered with sweat and hay, every muscle aching from lifting those heavy bales and tossing them around. There were nights when I did little more than shower, eat supper with my parents, and then go fall into the bed. If I stop and think about it, I can still remember how blissful and perfect it felt to be so tired, yet to be lying in a soft bed with a full stomach. I would wake up refreshed, and ready to do it all over again... I'd wake up restored.

Restoration is necessary in every living thing that exists on the earth. My grandfather had his own version of restoration. As a preacher, he always took Mondays off. That was a day of resting – and restoration – for him. Sometimes just being off wasn't enough, though. On occasion he loved to drive up into the Ozark mountains, which he found to be a place of beauty and solitude. On those particular Monday mornings he'd get up early, and wake the family up by loudly singing the old song, "Far away places, with strange sounding names..." That was a signal to the family that it was time to jump up and get dressed in a hurry, because the car would soon be rolling toward the Ozarks. My Mother would help Grandmother pack a picnic lunch for the day, and they'd be off for a relaxing day trip into the mountains. I'm told that Granddad would often stop the car at a roadside park, and just get out and look at the beauty and majesty surrounding him. After a day like that, I'm sure that he was ready to go back and tackle any problems that might be waiting... he was restored.

All these things are wonderful, but what the Psalmist is really talking about in verse three is not the type of physical restoration that I experienced after a day in the hay fields, or Granddad did with a drive through the Ozark mountains. Instead, this verse is speaking of a restoration of your soul.

Throughout the ages, philosophers and theologians much more intelligent than I have tried to divide the human being into different parts, some of which they classify as body, mind, heart, soul, spirit, etc.

I've always felt like there are only two halves to each of us – a physical self and a spiritual self, or soul. I think that the difference in the two is clear. For example, I was reading an article by the Regenerative Medicine Organization the other day, and it said that our bodies replace about 10% of our bone mass each year. That means that in a 75-year-old man, the average age of his bones is only seven years. Similar facts are true about our organs, our tissues, and every cell in our body.

Now – close your eyes and think of a childhood memory. Seriously, do it now, before you read any further.

Did you think of one? Good. I flashed back to a memory of my grandmother cooking fried chicken after church on Sunday morning. When I was young, they would invite my parents and me over for a delicious meal nearly every Sunday. I can still smell the chicken frying, and taste the white gravy on a piece of fresh bread. It was a wonderful experience, and we'd all enjoy the fellowship and good food.

Now, the thing about it is, not a single cell in my body that I have today was present then, and the same is true for you and your own memory that you thought of. The physical you of today was simply *not there*. Your body has regenerated, yet that picture is still very clear in your mind. Some scientists might contend that the memory is simply an electrical impulse bouncing around in a brain, but I'm not sure how it could have survived if there wasn't something else to it. In fact, the Bible indicates that it is something very different. Romans 14:12 speaks of Heaven: *"So then each of us shall give account of himself to God."* If we must give a personal account of our lives to God after our death, we must have the memories of our mortal life when we are in heaven, just like the childhood memory that you thought of a moment ago. To me, that means that such thoughts more than electrical signals – they're part of our spiritual self... our soul.

Matthew 25:34-40 further illustrates this: *"Then shall the King say unto them on his right hand, Come, ye blessed of my Father, inherit the kingdom prepared for you from the foundation of the world: For I was an hungred, and ye gave me meat: I was thirsty, and ye gave me drink: I was a stranger, and ye took me in: Naked, and ye clothed me: I was sick, and ye visited me: I was in prison, and ye came unto me. Then shall the righteous answer him, saying, Lord, when saw we thee an hungred, and fed thee? or thirsty, and gave thee drink? When saw we thee a stranger, and took thee in? or naked, and clothed thee? Or when saw we thee sick, or in prison, and came unto thee? And the King shall answer and say unto them, Verily I say unto you, Inasmuch as ye have done it unto one of the least of these my brethren, ye have done it unto me."* Clearly, in this passage the righteous people in Heaven state that they didn't do any of the things that the Savior is acknowledging in them: that they fed Him, clothed Him, etc. They have looked back at their mortal lives, searching their memories, which these verses indicate they have retained even in Heaven.

When I therefore think of our souls needing restoration, I look at the non-physical part of us – the thinking, feeling, emotional, spiritual self. Just like I remember lying in bed after

27

hauling hay all day, I can think back to many times throughout my life when I was also aching – not physically, but spiritually. Perhaps a time when someone had said something hurtful to me, or I'd done something for which I felt guilty. Maybe I was having physical problems that concerned me and gave me mental anguish and worry. At one time or another in my life, I've experienced all these and more... the kind of things that make you toss and turn all night, and fret about every moment of the day. These are the times when God is prepared to restore the soul, as the Psalmist is referring to in this verse, and it is as wonderful and recharging as the meal and soft bed were to my aching muscles after a day in the hay fields.

There was a time not that long ago when a company that I was a partner in was purchased by a larger firm. It seemed like a great opportunity for everyone around. The larger company would acquire our assets, inventory, and expertise, along with our payable and receivable accounts. We would get a nice financial compensation, and would be retained as consultants. It was a wonderful deal, until after a while when the checks stopped showing up on time – a week late here, a month there, dwindling down to no checks at all. We were given excuses and promises instead, but by the time that we realized how empty these promises were, it was too late. All of our liquid assets were gone, and we discovered that not only had the larger firm stopped sending us our money, but they'd done the same with our accounts payable months before. Our company and individual credit was trashed, and all that we had to show for years of building a successful business was the inventory that we were able to take back. It was a terribly dark time in my life. I felt hurt, angry, helpless, forlorn, and as much as I don't want to admit it, I felt pure hatred for the larger firm and the people associated with it. I couldn't sleep at night, and as far as I could see there was no way out of the hole that we'd found ourselves in. The pain was so bad that I'd literally sit by myself and cry.

But that's not the end of my story.

I found my way out of the darkness by the promises that God gives us in the 23rd Psalm. I knew that by claiming his words, I wouldn't have to want. I wouldn't have anything to fear. And for all the people that I was so afraid to face – people we did business with, suppliers, even our creditors, I would have a table set for me in their presence, and God would shower me with His favor and blessings. There was a problem, though. I still had all that pent-up anger and rage, and before I could move on to all the good things that He had in store for me, I was first going to have to allow God to restore my soul.

As hard as it was, I forgave the people who had wronged me. I opened myself up to the fact that although I couldn't possibly see how, everything would be all right. I tried to let go of all the fear and worry, and instead focus on the fact that we would somehow rebuild the company. All that didn't happen overnight; it took time. It took me saying each verse aloud, every single day, and dwelling on the 23rd Psalm whenever I felt vulnerable – and not just reciting the words, but embracing their meaning. Even when I woke up dreaming of our troubles, I would lie back down and go over the verses in my head. Little by little, I felt better. I was happier, I was encouraged, I was hopeful... and my soul was restored.

Since that time, we've continued to slowly rebuild the company. Although we have a long ways to go, we're going in directions that we could have never imagined before. We are using marketing techniques that we had never thought of, and the future is extremely bright. Every day I see God's promises in the 23rd Psalm being fulfilled in that company, not to mention my life as a whole.

When I do my daily meditation on the 23rd Psalm and I get to the verse that says, "He restoreth my soul," I know exactly what it means, and it continues to bring me a sense of peace, just like it will for you.

29

Chapter 6: The Paths Of Righteousness

He Leadeth Me In The Paths Of Righteousness For His Name's Sake. Imagine that you're buying something at the local grocery store, and the checkout person hands you back five dollars too much in change, and then begins to walk away... A meeting at work started five minutes ago, but before slowing down in the school zone that you're driving through, you glance around and there isn't a police car in sight... A new store is opening at the mall with some incredible sales, but you don't want to use a vacation day to go – it would be so much easier to call in sick...

These kinds of things are at the root of this verse; the righteousness that the Psalmist is talking about is simply doing what is right and correct. This verse plainly states that He leads in the right path, and we should follow it for the glory of His name.

Everyone knows what's right and wrong; whenever we have a decision to make, we feel it in our gut. Some people would say that our conscious is calling to us in such times, but to be honest, I think that it is this verse of the Psalm in action. I believe that God is trying to lead us in the path of righteousness.

Like a sheep, though, we don't necessarily *have* to follow. We can make our own choices and follow our own path, but if we do so, we have to live with the consequences. While God freely forgives us when we ask, the results of the paths that we have chosen in the past are still part of our lives.

When I think back to things that I might regret in my own life, things that I'd change if I ever had the chance, I recall one morning many years ago. I was caught up in the corporate world and as I left the house, my mind was already on projects

31

and deadlines looming over my head. There were pressures at work that already seemed to be closing in on me even though I wasn't even there yet, so I focused only on getting to my job that morning. As I drove along, I looked up to see a disabled car stopped in my lane, and I threw on my brakes while simultaneously glancing over my left shoulder to see if I could move over. Seeing that it was clear, I swerved around it, cursing the driver under my breath for leaving the car right out in the middle of the road. As I sped back up, something happened that I've never said aloud before, nor shared with another living soul. I was thinking that someone was going to hit that car if it wasn't moved, and as I glanced back into my rear-view mirror, I saw another automobile plow into it at full speed. I should have turned immediately around and gone to help out, but instead, all that I could think about was my job and my perceived responsibilities there. I didn't want to be late and get into trouble.

Writing those words is the first time that I've admitted that. I didn't tell the folks at work, or any of my friends, and not even my wife. As my loved ones read this book, it will be the first that they hear of this, and I feel horribly ashamed. I have no idea whether the victim of that crash was hurt, or even whether they lived or died, but as I sped away to work, I dismissed the incident by thinking, "surely that person had an airbag" and "someone else will stop and help."

It should have been me who helped, though. I should have turned around immediately and offered aid to that person who I know must have been hurt in the crash. I wasn't walking in the paths of righteousness, though – I was worried about my job, my salary, and the personal concerns of my own life. Years later, when I came to grips with what a terrible person I'd been and asked forgiveness for such a horrible act, I know that I was immediately forgiven... but in my mind I still wonder what happened to that person in the crash, and what kind of difference that I might have made if only I'd been following the path of righteousness that God wanted for me. Perhaps I was supposed to be His tool that day to help the person, and I simply ignored the opportunity. Maybe I could have saved a life. I don't know... it's something that I'll carry with me for as long as I live. I can close my eyes and still see it happen in the rear-view mirror.

As I said before, He might lead us in the path of righteousness for His name's sake, but if we choose to go otherwise, even though we're forgiven, we have to live with the consequences of our choices.

The 23rd Psalm is not a visit to a cafeteria; you can't pick and choose from its verses. While we are calling on God to fulfill our needs, protect and bless us, it is also important to consider the words of this verse and their meaning. He leads us in the path of righteousness – not the paths of evil, vanity, gossip, selfishness, anger or hate, but instead the paths of honesty, morality, decency, virtue and justice.

I really don't want to sound preachy, but this is one of the truths about the 23rd Psalm... how can one knowingly lead an immoral life, and still call on the Lord's blessings? You cannot declare, "The Lord is my shepherd, I shall not want," and then *not* follow the paths of righteousness that He has laid out for your life.

If you are reading this book, I doubt very seriously that you are a murderer on the run from the law, or have been the mastermind behind a series of unsolved bank heists across the nation. That doesn't mean that you are walking in the path of righteousness, however. You may say, "I am a good person," and then follow it up with, "but everyone cheats on their income tax." Or how about, "I'm a respected businessperson, but it's a cut-throat world out there, and I have to make under-the-table deals – everyone expects that." Perhaps even, "I may tend to gossip a little, but hey, I still go to church every Sunday."

I remember going places around my hometown with my

Granddad as a kid. Until I was old enough to attend Elementary School, my grandparents kept me while my Dad was at work and my Mother taught school. Few kids are that lucky, but I was. Not only did he teach me how to fish, but he pretty much took me along whenever he had to leave the house. There were daily errands to fulfill – checking the mail at the Post Office, going to the grocery store, or stopping by any number of other places around town. I distinctly remember times that we would walk into a place where men were conversing, and once they noticed us, would quickly shush each other's words and stories and give a slight nod toward Granddad; a preacher was suddenly present.

On one particular day that I recall, we went into a small grocery in my hometown. A grocer was behind the counter, and several men were leaning over on it, or reclining on the soft drink boxes beside it. Quite a conversation must have been taking place. As Granddad and I walked through the front door, whatever words they were saying abruptly stopped, and their smiles were frozen on their faces like they'd been caught with their hands in the cookie jar.

Even at such a young age, I knew that the silence was extremely awkward for everyone... except Granddad, of course. He just smiled and started talking about the weather or something else that would put everyone at ease. But I knew that he was completely aware that some other topic had been being discussed.

It was so strange to me because I remember wondering what they could have been talking about that they wouldn't want my grandfather to hear, but I figured that it was obviously something important.

As an adult, looking back, I can't possibly follow their logic – if they were telling an off-color or prejudicial joke, or spreading some steamy gossip, it didn't matter a bit whether my Grandfather heard it or not, since he certainly wasn't their judge. God, who sees and hears everything, was privy to their conversation long before we walked through the door. Like Number 32:23 says, *Be sure your sin will find you out!*

That can be a very disturbing verse to contemplate – no matter how hard you might try, you can't hide your sins. No matter what you may be tempted to do, no matter how well-concealed something might be, remember that your sin will eventually come out into the open.

Thomas Jefferson gave some excellent advice on the subject: "Whenever you do a thing, act as if the whole world was watching." And basically, that's what you have to do. You can declare, *"The Lord is my shepherd; I shall not want,"* and follow that with a heartfelt conviction that He makes you lie down in green pastures and leads you beside the still waters. You can even claim His restorative power on your soul. When you say, *"He leadeth me in the paths of righteousness for his name's sake,"* however, that is between you and God, and He knows your heart even better than you do. The world may see you as a leader in your community, but God knows the real you, including your innermost thoughts and secrets. He knows how you go about living your life.

In the deepest recesses of your soul, you may think, "Sure, I've cheated on my spouse a few times, but I've been careful – no one will ever find out." Or maybe your downfall is business; some of the most upstanding Christians are ruthless in that arena, and are proud of it: "It may have been a shady business deal, but not only did I bring profit to my company, I also left our competitor in the dust!" It could even be something small and seemingly insignificant: "I know that it's illegal to copy these movies I rented, but everyone does it – no one cares!"

No matter what you think, say or do, remember that man will see you only from the outside. Although that outside appearance may be squeaky-clean, God knows what is inside you. I Samuel 16:7 says, *for the Lord seeth not as man seeth;*

35

for man looketh on the outward appearance, but the Lord looketh on the heart.

Not that any of us are perfect – we all fall prey to sin. Romans 3:10 states: *There is none righteous no, not one.* And I'm sure that you're familiar with Romans 3:23: *For all have sinned, and come short of the glory of God.*

Thankfully, it is not a hopeless condition for anyone. When we do stray from the paths of righteousness, I John 1:9 says: *If we confess our sins, he is faithful and just to forgive us our sins and to cleanse us from all unrightousness.*

The task is not just to be forgiven for the times that you fall – the Lord is ready, willing and able to do that the moment that you confess and repent. Instead, the task is to make His path of righteousness the rule, and not the exception. It is saying on a daily basis, "Lord, with your help today, I'm going to walk in your path of righteousness."

From where I sit today, would I handle the car wreck situation differently? You bet – I would immediately turn around and minister aid, and wait until the entire situation was resolved. And if anyone at work was angry because I stopped to do that, it wouldn't cause me a moment's worry. But you know what they say about hindsight – it's 20/20. Since I didn't do any of those things, I'll continue to see the wreck in my mind, and wonder what happened to the person – or persons – in the car. I wasn't following the path of righteousness.

What I can say to you today, though, is to live the path of righteousness. You will stumble, but we all do. Sometimes you'll not only stumble, but will take a head-over-heels, double-summersault spill… but that's okay. The forgiveness of the Lord is immeasurable, and He will be there to pick you up, dust you off, and put His arm around you. What is important is that you continue to focus on the paths of righteousness where the Lord is leading you. Before you can claim any of the blessings of the 23rd Psalm, in your heart you must be able to claim this verse as well.

Chapter 7: The Valley Of The Shadow

Yea, though I walk through the valley of the shadow of death, I will fear no evil: for thou art with me. If you walk through a dark valley with the mountains towering high around, you know that you'll eventually come out beyond it – but the walk through can be terrifying. This verse deals with the fear of crossing through such a valley, and I believe that by using the particular words that he did, the Psalmist is first and foremost referring to physical death. When we were talking about fears back in the "still waters" chapter, I purposefully left out any discussion on the fear of death, because it is addressed in the Psalm by its very own verse – the fear of death is that significant.

Fear of death is one of the most common and intense fears of mankind. No matter where you go in the world, no matter what the culture, you will find that people have a fear of death.

Psychologists tell us that there are several reasons for this fear. First of all, death is the ultimate unknown – and each one of us must die. Hebrews 9:27 says, *And as it is appointed unto men once to die.* There's no way out of it, and no escaping it. It is mysterious, and something that none of us have experienced before; that bit of the unknown can cause great dread.

The second reason for fearing death is that of facing God. That same verse, Hebrews 9:27, concludes with: *but after this the judgment.* Even the most devoted Christians have at one time or another had doubts about facing God in judgment. Mother Teresa's biography contains letters that she wrote wrestling with her own faith, even though she is recognized as an icon of Christianity.

The third aspect of the fear of death is that of being completely and totally alone. Even though your entire family might be standing beside your deathbed, praying and holding your hand when you die, we often think of having to make that crossing over alone – and that prospect can be terrifying. Even though the Lord has promised to always be with us, to never forsake us, our mortal selves cannot help but look at death as a lonely path... which, of course, is the heart of what this verse is all about.

Finally, people fear death because it can come at any time. Young folks often think of death as something to worry about when they get old, and try to push it out of their minds for as long as they can. That's not realistic, though. I knew a young man who seemed to have a long, prosperous life ahead of him. He was the picture of health: he got a physical every year, exercised regularly, and didn't smoke or eat fatty foods. This fellow had a wonderful family, a great job, and was respected and loved by everyone. One day he was driving down the road and his car was hit by an out of control automobile from the other lane. He never regained consciousness; in a very short time, he was dead. Death discriminates against no one; we will all die, and we have no idea when or how.

The Psalmist has chosen a powerful image for this verse: the valley of the shadow of death. Thankfully, death *at its worst* is only a shadow. We've all heard the old expression, "don't be afraid of your shadow," an old colloquialism meaning that we shouldn't be afraid of inconsequential things like our own shadow. I'm sure that you can recall a time when you've been walking down a dark street with no one else around, and you start wondering whether someone is going to leap out of the darkness and assault you. You probably flinched at every little sound, and were scared every time you thought that you saw a shadow move by. I'd bet that when you came to the end of the street, perhaps to your car, or your house, or whatever destination was your safe haven, you probably laughed at how nervous you were over nothing. In that same manner, I'm sure that after we have died and conquered death through the mercy and glory of Jesus Christ, we will probably each look back and say, "Is that what I was afraid of?" Think of the words of Paul, who in I Corinthians 15:55 declared, *Death, where is thy sting? O grave, where is thy victory?*

My Granddad observed this about death:

"I have conducted many funerals, and each one of them became a new experience for me. Seven times I have faced the experience in my own family: my father, my mother, three brothers, one sister, and a little boy of my own. With each experience God was with me in a strengthening and comforting way, bringing to my mind and heart what He says about death and life in the Bible."

Remember that death is not the destination, but simply the journey – the means by which we pass into Heaven… into glory. I'm not saying that the sentiment helps that much, since I've cried at many funerals, including my Granddad's. But I do find comfort in the fact that they now know a place that I can't even imagine.

I recently took a trip to the west coast, and to get back home I had to fly through LAX, Los Angeles' world-famous airport. I wasn't looking forward to it one bit. I was a little anxious about flying in the post-9/11 world; I also knew that because security was so tight, getting checked in would be a major hassle. I imagined flight delays and a hundred other horrors. Throughout the entire the trip, I carried a little seed of dread in the back of my mind about the return trip home.

The last day came, and I took a cab to the airport. It dropped me right in front of the terminal, but then I had to stand at the end of a terribly long line that seemed to go on forever. "Here we go… the bad part starts now," I thought. In only a moment, an airport employee who was walking down the line checking tickets to make sure everyone was in the right place took mine, and said, "You already have everything set up – you can do self-check-in!" He pointed to a line leading to a bank of computer screens that was much shorter. I quickly moved over to it, checked in electronically, and then breezed through security. In no time at all I was sitting at a table in a coffee shop, reading a newspaper and waiting to board the plane. I couldn't help but laugh and think, "What the heck was I afraid of in the first place?

I believe that death will be like that – a lot of fear and worry before I get there, and then relief afterwards, as I shake my head and wonder what all the fuss was about. I think that's why this verse is in the Psalm: to assure us that through this situation of immense fear, God is with us.

Although I believe that this verse of the Psalm applies first to death, one of man's most dreadful fears, it can also apply to any fearful thing that we are going through in our lives. Think of what is scaring you:

"I don't want to go to the doctor for the test results, because I'm afraid of what he might say."

"I'm afraid to go to work this morning, because the company is having layoffs sometime this week."

"I can't stand to drive by the bank; I'm already two weeks late on the house payment."

No matter what you are going through, know that you will never be alone, as told in Romans 8:38-39: *neither death, nor life, nor angels, nor principalities, nor powers, nor things present, nor things to come, nor height, nor depth, nor any other creature, shall be able to separate us from the love of God, which is in Christ Jesus our Lord.*

Also, keep in mind what this verse actually says: "Yea, though I walk *through* the valley…" The Psalmist speaks here of a journey, not a destination. When the words of the 23rd Psalm describe an ending place, it is always somewhere wonderful: "green pastures," "still waters," and of course, "the house of the Lord." With all of the incredible places that God

40

has in store for each of us in our lifetime and beyond, this verse gives comfort for the rough passages that we will all have to occasionally face.

It assures us, though, that in the valley of the shadow of death, of debt, sickness, despair, worry, or trouble, you need not be afraid. Nothing can separate you from God's love, protection and comfort, and He will walk with you through whatever difficulty you might face.

The Valley Of The Shadow

Chapter 8: Thy Rod And Thy Staff

Thy rod and thy staff they comfort me. This is another verse that has a very strong visual image. The rod and staff were the essential tools of a shepherd, and the implements were commonplace and recognizable in that day and age. The rod was a straight stick, hearty, sometimes with a knob at one end; it was used as a weapon against the predators and enemies of the sheep. I think back to the fictional adventures of Robin Hood, and how proficient they were with the use of such a weapon in a fight – one particular scene between Friar Tuck and Little John on a tree trunk spanning a river comes to mind. In Biblical days, whether a person was a soldier or a shepherd, carrying the rod was a sign of authority and protection.

The staff was much different; where the rod was used for striking and bludgeoning an enemy, the staff was a gentler device. It was also a long stick, but had a large crook at one end that was just the perfect size to place around a sheep's neck to pull it back into the herd. Using the staff, a shepherd could move a sheep to fields of more grass, sources of water, and areas that offered better protection. The staff would allow him to steer the animal without hurting it, and as such, was a device of love and compassion.

Both the rod and the staff are mentioned as God's tools in this verse; but what does He do with them? The Psalmist says that He comforts His people – and it's important to note this duality of comfort that He provides: not only does He protect us from hazards, but He also steers us into areas of bounty and safety.

My wife and I lived in the Dallas area for about twenty years and I knew the Metroplex like the back of my hand. Thinking back to the very first time that I flew into the city for a job interview, however, it was quite an intimidating place. I got onto a bus at the airport – the wrong one as it turned out – and after about forty-five minutes found out that it didn't stop anywhere even close to my hotel. I was talking to the driver about options, and he suggested that I get off at the next stop, walk to the nearest hotel, and take a cab to my destination from there. Naively I did that, not realizing that I was being let off in a location where the closest hotel was six blocks away. It was night, and I found myself on a particularly seedy part of Industrial Boulevard, in a dangerous part of town. As the bus pulled away, all I could think about was that line from *The Wizard of Oz*: "Toto, we're not in Kansas anymore!" There were literally prostitutes on every street corner, and all sorts of unsavory characters along each block. Dressed in a suit and carrying a travel bag and briefcase, I probably looked like the easiest target in the world. The thought occurred to me that if only I had a police officer to escort me, I'd be perfectly safe. After all, he would probably know everyone on the street by name, and the bad guys would just fade into the darkness to keep from being noticed. If anyone did try any mischief, the officer would pull his gun in a heartbeat, and the police radio would bring a squadron of patrol cars. Without that protection, though, I simply whispered under my breath, "Lord, get me to that hotel safely." I did reach it, and caught a taxi to the place where I was staying. When I sat down safely in my room and thought back on the entire episode, I was amazed. As I walked along that dangerous thoroughfare, not a single one of the people around me gave me a glance. None of the working girls called out to me, their "business managers" didn't bother me, and in fact, no one paid any attention to me at all – it was if I was invisible, or somehow had that officer walking next to me. In retrospect, I know what happened, and it is described in this verse of the Psalm; the Lord was protecting me, armed in one hand with the rod of protection, and with the staff in the other, guiding me to safety. I couldn't help but think of the words of

Isaiah 41:13: *For I the Lord thy God will hold thy right hand, saying unto thee, Fear not; I will help thee.*

At the job interview, I told some of the people what had happened to me, and they stared in disbelief; a couple told me that I was lucky to even be alive because of all the crime concentrated in that area. If God was watching over me, then what trouble could befall me? I am again reminded of that powerful verse from Romans 8:31: *If God be for us, who can be against us?*

When you find yourself in a situation that is causing you to fear, claim the promises of this verse; ask for God's guidance and protection. When I was a kid, before we could go anywhere on a trip, we would always stand out in Granddad's front yard and he would lead us in a prayer for our safety. I remember one particular time that my mother and I were taking my grandmother to visit my aunt's family across the state of Texas. As always, my grandfather asked the Lord to protect us on the trip, unaware on this occasion that we would particularly need Him. We'd stopped to get gas along the way, and before getting back onto the Interstate my mother's car hit a slick spot on the service road and the car spun around three full times before coming to a screeching halt. There was silence in the car for a moment while we all caught our breath, but after Mother determined that everyone was okay, we laughed about it. I think that we were all grateful for God's comfort and protection, though – I know that I was. To this day I'm glad that Granddad insisted on starting out every trip with a prayer for safety.

The comfort that this verse offers isn't just in times when our safety is threatened, however. We are protected by the shepherd's rod, but we are also guided by the staff. That can be a simple nudging in the right direction, or a life change to take you on the path on which you're supposed to go.

There were many times in Granddad's life when he was shepherded by the staff of God, but one particular family story

45

leaps to mind. After he completed seminary, he took a position preaching at a church in Dallas. It was the time of the Great Depression, though, and life in the big city was harsh.

It wasn't just surviving in the urban setting that was a problem, though; my grandfather felt strongly like he was being led to be a country pastor and to help build up churches in small towns. He packed his family up, and moved back to rural East Texas. The economy may have been worse there than in the city, but he strongly felt like it was the place for him to be.

He found a church to pastor, even though they couldn't pay him a thing; everyone was struggling during those times. He was able to provide for his family, because he worked on his father-in-law's farm for a share of the proceeds. Granddad grew a garden to raise vegetables, and the members of the congregation shared meat and produce with him whenever they could.

On one particular day, Granddad was late in coming home. My mother and her siblings were watching for him to come walking down the railroad track, which was the shortest route to and from town. He finally appeared as a far-away speck, and as he got closer, they noticed that he was carrying a pail. This was something new, so they all ran out to meet him and find out what mystery awaited in the bucket. When they got there, the kids discovered that he had a gallon of sweet sorghum syrup. This was quite an unexpected treat, and they celebrated all the way home.

My grandmother was out on the front porch when they arrived to see what all the fuss was about, and as soon as Granddad told her, she grinned and said, "Let's make some biscuits!" A little while later, the family was gathered around the table enjoying an incredible treat: biscuits and syrup.

If you could look in on that scene right now, you probably wouldn't be all that impressed. It would appear for all purposes like a poor family who had been relegated to eating only biscuits for supper. In reality, though, it was one of the biggest treats for them in memorable times – a veritable feast! They all had a wonderful dinner of biscuits and sorghum syrup. That event has been handed down through my family over the years as the time that Granddad preached a year for a bucket of syrup.

I love that story; to me, it illustrates this verse perfectly. As Granddad moved his family away from the big city, he took a leap of faith, but he was being shepherded... and he was being protected. You've probably heard horror stories of urban life during the Depression, but he and his family were led away from that into a place that God would bless them. In fact, it was that very move that let him fulfill his role as a country preacher, building churches and congregations around rural East Texas.

This verse of the 23rd Psalm always brings comfort to me, and I believe that is its purpose in the scripture. It is a perfect illustration of the Lord's care, for the shepherd's rod protects you and the shepherd's staff guides you. For that reason, if I had to choose only one verse out of this Psalm to claim in my life, I believe that it would be this one... *Thy rod and thy staff they comfort me.*

Chapter 9: Thou Preparest
A Table

Thou preparest a table before me in the presence of mine enemies. When Granddad preached on the 23rd Psalm, he would often include a story: "One time a little boy had been misbehaving at dinner, and so his father said, 'Because you aren't acting correctly, you're going to have to leave the family table.' His mother set up a little tray over in the corner where the boy could eat by himself. His father said, 'Son, don't forget to thank the Lord for your food.' The little boy bowed his head, folded his hands together, and said, 'I thank you, Lord, for this meal and for preparing a table for me in the presence of my enemies!'"

I believe that he told that story not only because it was a cute little joke, but also because it illustrated this verse extremely well. The enemies referred to here certainly don't have to be people who you are at war with – they may simply be those that you are most uncomfortable around.

I also think it's significant that the Psalmist changed perspectives with this verse. The majority of the 23rd Psalm uses the analogy of a shepherd to his sheep; here, however, the scene changes to that of a host taking care of a special guest. By setting a table before you in the presence of your enemies, the Lord is going to make you comfortable in a most uncomfortable situation.

We are all occasionally thrust into situations that are not just uncomfortable, they're downright painful. We dread them, sidestep around them, and avoid them at all costs – yet God is willing to set a table for you in the middle of them as his honored guest!

I don't know of any enemies that my Granddad had in his life, or even anyone that he necessarily felt uncomfortable around. Still, I remember one story that might fit the bill for the Lord setting such a table for him.

If you speak with most any preacher – and they're being totally honest – you will find that if a point of contention is going to show up in the church, it is often between the pastor and the governing board of the church: the deacons, elders, etc.

At one point in his life, in his mid-fifties, he had been pastor of a particular church for over a decade, and a certain group in the church – including a few deacons – wanted to oust him and replace him with a younger man. As I now approach the age of fifty, I don't think that his age was all that old, and I personally would have resented it if I'd been in his shoes.

This was early in the calendar year, though, and the renegade deacons met with him and explained their plan to find a younger minister. Instead of fighting it, he accepted it as God's will for him to move on, and told them that he would resign on Sunday morning, if they would keep his contract through May – that way all of his children would finish the school year, and he would have the summer to secure another position. The deacons who were so bent on bringing in a youthful pastor agreed, and Granddad resigned that next Sunday morning. The church had to formally accept his resignation, so the congregation went into a business meeting after the service, and my grandparents, along with their children, had to file out and wait in a room while his fate was decided. I've been told that my Grandmother cried, and that everyone was a little confused by the whole thing – except for Granddad, of course. Finally, there was a knock on the door of the room where they were waiting, and they filed back into the sanctuary to find that his resignation had been accepted. The entire episode must have been unbelievably uncomfortable.

This again shows the highly spiritual nature of my grandfather – had it been me in his shoes, I might have spoken harshly to the congregation and stormed off in a huff. I would probably have shaken my first toward Heaven and said, "Lord,

I've been your servant; how can you treat me this way? Why aren't you protecting me from these people who are acting so ungrateful for all my hard work?"

Not Granddad, though. Even as my grandmother cried through the next few months, wondering what would happen to them after May, my Grandfather had only one thing to say on the subject: "God will provide."

Just think about how uncomfortable it must have been for him as he faithfully went about his work for the months left on his contract. To those that actively sought to oust him, he had to remain a compassionate pastor. To the church that was tossing him aside, he had to strive to be a servant. He did all those things, because in the presence of those who were against him, God had set a table.

His good nature never wavered, his devotion to the church never waned, even in the presence of adversity. He sat at the table that God had provided, and reveled in the blessing. Granddad knew that by serving out his term as pastor through May he would provide for his children through the school year, but he also knew that God was working in the background to provide something even greater.

In the same month that his contract was set to end, another church in a town not far away called him to be its pastor and it was there that he would spend the rest of his career. He helped build the congregation, literally constructed the church building with his hands, and will forever be remembered as a pioneer in that church. If the few deacons hadn't set out against him in the other congregation, though, he might have never found his new calling and the blessings that awaited him there.

God knew what He was doing, but during the transition phase, He made Granddad comfortable in an uncomfortable situation – He set a table for him in the presence of those who were against him.

I'm amazed how many times in my life this verse has

come into play; not that I necessarily have enemies, but I have found myself in uncomfortable situations before, as we all have. The Bible says in Psalm 118:6: *The Lord is on my side; I will not fear: what can man do unto me?* And Hebrews 13:6 says, *So that we may boldly say, The Lord is my helper, and I will not fear what man shall do unto me.* Though we may fear certain situations or even people, there is no harm that can befall us as a child of God.

There is another family story where the proverbial table wasn't set for Granddad, but instead for my Grandmother – Granddad just turned out to be the instrument of God. During his days as a preacher, the ladies of a church where he pastored were going to have a quilting. The wife in every family was supposed to sew a quilt square with their family name on it, and have it ready to start piecing and quilting one particular Saturday. There was only one problem – Grandmother couldn't sew. She could cook like a master chef, but sewing just wasn't a skill that she possessed. When Grandmother considered the prospect of appearing in front of all the ladies of the church that day and not being able to sew, she cried. All she could see was being humiliated in front of all of the churchwomen when they discovered that she couldn't sew.

Once Granddad found out what the problem was, he went in and sat down beside her, and explained that she had nothing to worry about. "You can cook, can't you?" he asked her. Grandmother acknowledged that she could certainly hold her own in the kitchen. He told her that he thought that he could sew a quilt square with the family name on it, so all she'd have to do was bring it, and while everything was getting started, she could get things going in the kitchen. After all, the quilting would take place in the church's Fellowship Hall, with the kitchen right beside it.

Granddad told her that she could get there and make coffee for the morning, then start preparing lunch and take care of serving it. During all the quilting time she'd be in and out of the room so much that everyone would assume that she was simply fulfilling a much-needed role that day... and her lack of sewing skills would never come to light.

Grandmother felt much better. She stopped crying, although she still probably dreaded the upcoming day. Their plan executed perfectly, though. She presented her quilt square to the ladies that morning, and then got busy in the kitchen. Floating around with refreshments, then lunch, and then tea for the afternoon, my grandmother was a constant presence at the quilting that day. The ladies probably considered her as much a part of it as anyone else. It wasn't just that she made it through the day, though – there was even something more special in store for her that even my Grandfather hadn't anticipated. As it turned out, the day was a surprise for my grandparents. The "congregation quilt" that the ladies were making was a gift, which they presented to Grandmother at the end of the day. God took an uncomfortable situation and turned it into even more of a blessing.

When I'm worrying about a situation, like my Grandmother was, I take solace in 1 Peter 3:12-13, which tells us that the eyes of the Lord watch over the righteous, and He listens to their prayers. It goes on to say that His face is against those who are evil, and concludes with: *who is he that will harm you, if ye be followers of that which is good?*

Who indeed can hurt you – who would dare, when God is setting a table for you in the presence of whatever enemies or situations that you will face throughout your life!

Chapter 10: Thou Anointest My Head

Thou anointest my head with oil. Sounds icky and a little gross, right? Maybe, but in this verse, the Psalmist is referring to the Biblical practice of pouring or rubbing oil into the skin – something that would be cool, soothing and refreshing in the heat of the desert. In fact, if I think about it, that might feel pretty good to me on a hot summer's day after I finished mowing the yard at my house.

This isn't just an issue of comfort, though; anointment was used in Biblical times for several other things. To understand what this verse is referring to, it is important to examine the concept of anointing.

First of all, anointment was used to purify, as explained in Exodus 29:36-37: *Sacrifice a bull each day as a sin offering to make atonement. Purify the altar by making atonement for it, and anoint it to consecrate it. For seven days make atonement for the altar and consecrate it. Then the altar will be most holy, and whatever touches it will be holy.* This is also shown in Leviticus 8:10, *Then Moses took the anointing oil and anointed the tabernacle and everything in it, and so consecrated them.*

The practice of anointing of the head was also used throughout the Old Testament to designate the offices of priests and kings. For example, when Samuel made Saul the first King over Israel, I Samuel 10:1 says, *Then Samuel took a vial of oil, and poured it upon his head, and kissed him, and said, Is it not because the Lord hath anointed thee to be captain over his inheritance?* The ceremony to consecrate priests is also explained in Exodus 29:7: *Take the anointing oil and anoint him by pouring it on his head.*

It was also used to honor a guest, and give them comfort from the heat of the day. In the New Testament, such a recognition was given to Jesus, as described in Matthew 26:6-10: *While Jesus was in Bethany in the home of a man known as Simon the Leper, a woman came to him with an alabaster jar of very expensive perfume, which she poured on his head as he was reclining at the table. When the disciples saw this, they were indignant. "Why this waste?" they asked. "This perfume could have been sold at a high price and the money given to the poor." Aware of this, Jesus said to them, "Why are you bothering this woman? She has done a beautiful thing to me."*

In this verse of the 23rd Psalm, not only has the Lord God prepared a table for you in the presence of your enemies, but he also anoints your head with oil – right there in front of those that you are most afraid of or are uncomfortable with, he calls you out as being honored, purified and special.

Before getting too comfortable at that table, however, you must realize something else: the anointing is also a preparation for service. As I pointed out earlier, the act of anointing symbolized priests, prophets and kings – all offices of service to their people. If you are to receive the gifts described in the 23rd Psalm, you have to be prepared to use them in the ways that God leads.

Don't forget the words of Luke 12:48: *For unto whomsoever much is given, of him shall be much required: and to whom men have committed much, of him they will ask the more.* Even though the 23rd Psalm speaks mainly of the many blessings that God wants to give us, this verse is a reminder that we have obligations as well.

In Matthew 25:14-29 Jesus tells the story of a master that was leaving on a trip, and gave three of his servants three different amounts of money which the Bible refers to as "talents". Upon his return, the master asked each what they had done with what he had given them. The first servant stepped up to show that he had taken the five talents that he was given, and increased them by five more. The master was delighted, and said, "Well done, good and faithful servant; you've been faithful over a few things, so I will make you the ruler over many more: enter into the joy of thy lord." The second servant came forward and showed that he had taken the two talents that he'd been given, and increased them by two more. The master was pleased, and gave him the same praise as the first servant. Finally the third servant showed the master that he had been given one talent, but since he was afraid of anything happening to it, he buried it in the ground for safekeeping. The master took the talent, but chastised the servant for being wicked and lazy, pointing out that at the very least he could have put it in the bank to gain interest – but he didn't even do that much. The master cast the third servant out into the darkness, and gave the talent to the first servant who already had ten. Matthew 25:29 concludes the story with the instruction, *For unto every one that hath shall be given, and he shall have abundance: but from him that hath not shall be taken away even that which he hath.*

When you think about this particular verse of the 23rd Psalm, understand that the anointing is a preparation for service. If you are anxious and ready to receive His blessings, you must also be prepared for the responsibilities that come with them. Remember that old adage: "Be careful what you ask for; you just might get it!"

If you pray for good health, and the Lord blesses you with it, what will you use your abilities for – are you ready to start helping others?

Perhaps your eyesight is failing and you ask for it to be restored – are you already making plans to read to children's groups at your local library, or commit books to audiotape for the elderly and blind? Like the servants who were given the talents in Jesus' example, if you expect blessings, you should already be planning on how to use them.

We all have expectations for our spouse, children, friends and co-workers. If someone in your life doesn't live up to your expectations, you probably notice it immediately. If someone that you work with isn't pulling their weight, you might have a word with them, but if the situation doesn't improve you could be forced to escalate the situation to the boss. If one of your children is doing something outside of your expectations, you might ground them or take away their cell phone for a week. In the same manner that we hold others accountable to our expectations, God holds us accountable for what we do – or don't do – with the gifts that He gives us. Be prepared to be blessed, but be ready to use the blessings that He gives you to help others.

There's a story in our family about the time that my grandparents finally got a car in their lives. They sold a house that Granddad built and used the money to buy a 1939 Dodge. Before then, the entire family walked everywhere that they went. As a pastor, he walked to visit sick members of the congregation and call on prospective new members for the church. My mother, aunts and uncles walked to school, and when the family went to any local store, they walked there as well. When the time came to make a trip into Texarkana, the nearest large city, the only option was a bus. You can imagine the excitement when the family could finally afford to get an automobile.

There weren't that many cars in their small town at the time – unlike today, very few people had them. My grandparents were blessed, and of course, Granddad used it to reach out even more to the congregation.

A young couple lived in the house behind them; the man was an Army veteran who had met his wife in New England, and they had settled in East Texas. His wife was expecting their first child, and was having a tough time since all of her family was in New England; she was emotional and distressed.

Gas cost money, of course, which was a commodity that my grandparents still didn't have an abundance of. When they learned of their neighbor's situation, though, my grandparents went to visit them. They insisted that when the time came to go to the hospital, the couple call them instead of waiting for the bus. It would be an extra burden, both of time and of money, but my grandfather knew that whoever was given much, much would be expected from – but he also knew that the Lord would provide. In the next few months, they made not just one, but three trips to the hospital with the couple and child.

I don't know what happened to that young couple, but it's possible that their child grew up and had children, and then they had children, and the next generation had even more children. For whatever reason, God gave my Granddad a car so that the couple could go straight to the hospital without having to struggle with the bus; who knows what incredible plans were put into motion by that simple action.

All I do know is that even though Granddad was made to be special with the acquisition of a car, he was anointed to do special jobs with it as well.

When you read this verse, remember the many meanings of being anointed with oil: you are being honored, you are being consecrated, but you are also being selected for service. Don't worry, though, because as you fulfill the services in which God leads, you will be blessed even more.

Chapter 11: My Cup Runneth Over

My Cup Runneth Over. This is perhaps one of the most reassuring verses in the Psalm; it is not difficult to close your eyes and see a cup on a table, with someone pouring water into it until it literally overflows onto the tabletop.

Of course, the cup or vessel referred to here is you – and the thing that is overflowing are the blessings that God wants to bestow on you: spiritual blessing, life, redemption, forgiveness, peace, joy and prosperity, to name but a few. How? That's easy; let's take a look at just a few of the ways that the Lord wants your cup to overflow…

Your cup overflows with all spiritual blessings. Ephesians 1:3 assures us of this: *Blessed be the God and Father of Lord Jesus Christ, who hath blessed us with all spiritual blessings in heavenly places in Christ.* These spiritual blessings include redemption, forgiveness, peace of mind, and restoration of your soul – nothing will God withhold from you.

Your cup overflows with life. In John 10:10 Christ said, *I am come that they might have life, and that they might have it more abundantly.* To live is the greatest of all blessings. I love to live – to me, life is exciting and wonderful, and I thank the Lord for letting me be alive. God doesn't want an ordinary life for any of us, though; he wants our lives to be abundant with all things.

Your cup overflows with redemption. In Revelation 5:9 this overflowing of redemption is described by the words: *And they sung a new song, saying, Thou art worthy to take the book, and to open the seals, thereof: for thou wast slain and has redeemed us to God.* That passage describes Jesus' sacrifice that was made for us, and the fact that with it he bought redemption – an eternal place of glory and bounty, even though we aren't worthy.

Your cup overflows with forgiveness. Jeremiah 31:34 reads: *Saith the Lord: for I will forgive their iniquity, and I will remember their sin no more.* That exact sentiment is echoed in Hebrews 10:17 where these words are found: *And their sins and iniquities will I remember no more.* Note that it's not a simple forgiveness. I may forgive someone for slighting me in a business deal, but every time I have contact with him I'll still think, "I remember what a terrible thing he did to me." God's forgiveness is not like that – His forgiveness overflows. He forgives our sins, and it is if they never existed.

Your cup overflows with peace. John 14:27 states, *Peace I leave with you, my peace I give unto you: not as the world giveth, give I unto you. Let not your heart be troubled, neither let it be afraid.* Your heart may be a raging sea of doubts, fear, and anxiety. But there is peace – great peace, that passes all understanding… your cup will run over with that peace.

Your cup overflows with joy. In John 15:11 Christ reminds us that, *These things I have spoken unto you, that my joy might remain in you, and that your joy might be full.* One can be robbed of his money, his good name, his friends, but not his joy in the Lord. My wife came home one day after work and found me whistling a tune while I did the dishes. She said, "You must have had a wonderful day – what happened to put you in such a good mood?" I told her that I'd lost a major account, and it was really a significant blow. She looked puzzled and asked, "Then why are you so happy?" I just smiled and said, "For God to have shut that door so swiftly and suddenly, he must be getting ready to rain down a blessing on me that the account was interfering with, and I can hardly wait to find out what it is!" Joy can always be found when your cup is running over.

These are merely few ways that your cup can overflow. Stop for a moment and embrace this verse – God wants your cup to overflow in all things. For example, II Kings 4:1-7 has a wonderful story of a person's cup flowing over. A woman came to see the prophet Elisha and told him that her husband had died, and the family was in so much debt that the creditors were knocking on the door for the money that was owed. They were even going to take her two sons into slavery to pay the debt. Elisha asked what they had in the house, and the distraught woman answered, "Nothing, except a pot of oil." The prophet instructed her to return home, and to borrow pots, pans, and all manner of containers from her neighbors – not just a few, but as many as she could find. He then said that she and her sons should go into their house and shut the door, and start pouring oil from their pot into all of the other containers that they borrowed. The woman did just that, but found that something incredible was happening... all the jars were being filled, but their own pot wasn't running out of oil. They continued until all of the borrowed vessels were full. The woman ran back to Elisha and told him what had happened, and he instructed her to sell the surplus of oil and pay the debt, and then live off the rest of the money that was raised.

The widow was given a miracle from God to rescue them from their financial straits. What was required of her first, though, was that she had to have the faith to trust in the unlikely and unbelievable instructions that have been given to her. Sometimes that can be the hardest task of all – having faith when the problems seem insurmountable. She did, though, and look at what happened; her debts were erased, and she had an abundance of money to live on.

Granddad's life always seemed to be overflowing. I remember one particular story in our family about a time not long after the Great Depression, when my grandfather was a pastor of a church in a small East Texas town. He had two white shirts: a new, good one, and an older one that had been around for a while. He wore the new one every Sunday to preach in, and the older one he wore during the week to do visitations and minister to the members of the congregation. One day, a man came by with a request: he had finally managed to get a job interview, and needed a white shirt to wear. My grandfather went back to his closet and retrieved the best one of the two, the new one that he kept for Sunday morning services. The man thanked him, took it, and left. After that, my Grandmother was shocked; she asked him, "Why didn't you give him the old one – it would work just as well." Granddad just said, "I could never do that; I had to give him my best." Soon thereafter a family from the church came into a little extra money. They thought that as a pastor, Granddad might need some extra changes of nice clothing, so they bought him two brand new shirts from J.C. Penny. Suddenly there were three shirts in his closet – in post-Depression America, his cup was truly running over.

That is the promise that God has for you in this verse; not only will He meet your needs, but your cup will overflow with His blessings.

Chapter 12: Surely Goodness And Mercy

Surely goodness and mercy shall follow me all the days of my life. I was out for my morning walk the other day, and saw a dog trotting across its yard toward me. Our city doesn't have any leash laws, so although I'm not a big fan of the practice, many people let their pets run free. This particular dog seemed to be nice enough, and just fell in step behind me. As we got further away from his home turf I kept turning around and saying, "Go home, boy – go on back." He kept plodding along after me, though, and did so for several blocks. That's not the kind of "follow" that I believe that the Psalmist was referring to in this verse; I think that it's just the opposite, in fact. One chilly Friday evening last Fall I was watching a local high-school football game, and on one play our town's running back was shooting down the field like a streak, the football tucked under his arm. Right behind him, though, was the defensive tackle intent on catching him; the tackle following every bob and swerve of the runner like a shadow. God's goodness and mercy – His undying, boundless generosity and love – doesn't loosely follow us like that hapless hound roaming the streets that I described. Instead, it pursues us, runs behind us, and is constantly at our heels like that defensive tackle.

Look back at the first word of this verse: surely. The Psalmist didn't say, "sometimes," "occasionally," or even "under the right circumstances, goodness and mercy will follow me." He said the emphatic word "surely". That is a definitive: *Certainly*, beyond any shadow of a doubt, without question, no matter what else happens, goodness and mercy shall follow you all the days of your life. You can't escape it; you can't outrun it; you can't hide from it.

Baseball legend Leroy "Satchel" Paige once observed, "Don't look back – something may be gaining on you!" In this verse, we can be comforted by what really is gaining on us: God's promise of a life filled with goodness and mercy.

Deuteronomy 28:2 underscores the sentiment of this verse of the 23rd Psalm: *And all these blessings shall come on thee, and overtake thee, if thou shalt hearken unto the voice of the Lord thy God.* Blessings will not only follow you, but they will chase and engulf you.

There are times in everyone's lives when we feel alone and abandoned. We may look over our shoulder and wonder where the goodness and mercy are. Like our Lord in Matthew 27:46, we may even be tempted to call out, *My God, my God, why hast thou forsaken me?*

God loves you, though, and is arranging the world around you for your benefit, letting His goodness and mercy overtake you. Sometimes, though, that may take a little time. Habakkuk 2:3 says: *For the vision is yet for an appointed time, but at the end it shall speak, and not lie: though it tarry, wait for it; because it will surely come, it will not tarry.*

The goodness and mercy that God has for you will not tarry – it won't delay – one microsecond more than is necessary for His plan for you to come to fruition. You must be patient, though, and hold close this verse of the Psalm. God's goodness and his mercy are following close behind you as you journey through life.

My grandfather had been called to pastor a church in a small East Texas town; the church very much wanted him, and he felt led to accept their invitation. The only problem was that this was the 1930's, and times were hard. The church could only promise him ten dollars a month, and he had a family to provide for. As much as he lived the promises of the 23rd Psalm, Granddad must have been wondering where God's goodness and mercy were. As it turned out, both were chasing him – pursuing him – without him knowing what wonderful things were in store.

He accepted the position of pastor of the church on the faith in the promises that are spelled out in this verse... and that's when things began to happen. One of the deacons owned a rent house, and came to see Granddad and offered to let him have it for five dollars a month. Next, my grandfather found out that they could have electricity at the house for only $1.50 a month – still well within their budget. Since he had handmade all their furniture years ago, the family already had all of the furnishings that they needed. Everything fell right into place... and the blessings kept coming.

One member of the congregation began to stop by every Saturday and bring my grandparents two chickens. Another member would bring by a basket of corn, still another would come to drop off a bushel of peas. Although it might have initially seemed impossible, with the blessings of the Lord, Granddad was able to provide for his family. Even though he didn't know how it would happen, my grandfather believed in the words of this verse. Sure enough, goodness and mercy chased him down and overtook him – I think one of the reasons that he loved the 23rd Psalm was its constant proof of God's words in his life, just as it will be in yours.

67

Chapter 13: In The House Of The Lord

...and I will dwell in the house of the Lord for ever. I mentioned how powerful the opening verse to the 23rd Psalm is, but perhaps the one that closes it is even more so. Every word and line of the Psalm – with the exception of this last one – describes God's relationship with you on Earth: He wants to provide for you, protect you, and lift you up. These last words, however, go beyond our mortal existence; they describe your life after death.

We've talked about the fear of death and the valley of the shadow, but that is a human fear present only on Earth. This verse explains what happens once we have experienced death, and walked through that door.

But what is the house of the Lord – Heaven – really like? Well, I remember sitting in church as a youngster listening to the preacher give a sermon on the very subject of Heaven. He said that it would be filled with huge choir lofts, and that we'd spend every minute for the rest of eternity singing hymns. With a big smile, he added, "Won't that be wonderful?"

I remember thinking, "NO!" Words can't describe how appalled I was by that prospect, because I didn't want to sit in a choir loft singing hymns out of the church songbook forever – I wasn't sure that I wanted any part of Heaven at all.

Many years later, I was visiting with a friend and we were just sitting out on his porch musing about life on a lazy afternoon. The subject of Heaven somehow came up, and I asked him, "So what do you think it's like there?"

He just kind of looked off into the distance for a few minutes, and finally turned back to me. "I don't really know... but I do know this. Imagine the most perfect day of your life so far – the one day that you'll always remember as the best time you've ever had. Well, Heaven's going to be a whole lot better than that."

I don't think any Bible scholar or philosopher could have put it any better. It's a description of Heaven that I'll carry with me throughout my life, until I actually get to set foot there.

Looking to the Bible, though, there are many glimpses of Heaven and what it will be like.

First and foremost, it is critical to understand that Heaven is a place for Christians – those who have accepted Jesus as their personal savior and believe in Him. In John 11:25-26, Jesus was comforting Martha on the death of her brother Lazarus: *Jesus said unto her, I am the resurrection, and the life: he that believeth in me, though he were dead, yet shall he live: And whosoever liveth and believeth in me shall never die.*

Jesus also assures us that such a place as Heaven exists. In John 14:2, He says: *In my Father's house are many mansions: if it were not so, I would have told you. I go to prepare a place for you.*

Heaven will be much better than our Earthly existence. In his letter to the church at Philippi, Paul says, *for to me to live is Christ, but to die is gain* – Philippians 1:21. This gain is getting to spend all eternity in the presence of the Lord, his angels, and all other Christians who have gone on before us – we will never be alone. Hebrews 12:22-23 gives this account of Heaven: *But ye are come unto mount Sion, and unto the city of the living God, the heavenly Jerusalem, and to an innumerable company of angels, To the general assembly and church of the firstborn, which are written in heaven, and to God the Judge of all, and to the spirits of just men made perfect.* One afternoon I was sitting at my desk working, and I stopped to reflect on how wonderful life was. We were going out to eat with friends that evening, my parents had been in town for a visit just a few days before, and I knew that my wife would be coming through the door in just a short while. I felt so rich to be surrounded by people who love me. Life seemed so perfect at that moment that I remember thinking, "Why can't things be like this forever?" In reality, I think that it will be, but in a place that's even better than I could imagine.

Heaven will also be a place of rest – there will be no more time clocks, deadlines, or laborious jobs. Most people can relate to that idea, since almost everyone looks forward to retirement, when they can just take it easy and enjoy the golden years of life. The rest from labor also follows you to heaven, because Revelation 14:13 says: *Blessed are the dead which die in the Lord from henceforth: Yea, saith the Spirit, that they may rest from their labours; and their works do follow them.*

It will be a joyous place as well, for Revelation 21:4 describes it by saying: *And God shall wipe away all tears from their eyes; and there shall be no more death, neither sorrow, nor crying, neither shall there be any more pain: for the former things are passed away.* Can you imagine a place with no worries, no pain, and no tears? Everyone has encountered hardship and trouble in their life, but in Heaven, such concepts simply will not exist.

The Bible gives many other vignettes of Heaven, but even so, I don't think that it is a place that we can truly grasp with the limits of our current minds. There's one story that I always think of when I'm contemplating Heaven, though. My Dad loves to tell about a vacation before I came along where he and Mother hit the road toward the Southwest with my grandparents. One stop on the agenda was the Grand Canyon, but my Granddad was complaining the entire way there. "I don't want to go see an old hole in the ground," he'd say. That was his assessment of the beautiful place that is considered to be one of the seven wonders of the natural world.

The closer that they got, the more he complained. When they finally arrived, my Grandfather was suddenly intrigued. He got out of the car, slowly walked over to the edge of the canyon and just soaked in its magnificence. For what was probably one of the few times in his life, he was totally speechless. After a long period of silence, he finally said, "Well, well, well... what do you know about that." Granddad was impressed.

That's how I think that I'll be about Heaven. I was raised on stories of streets paved gold and lined with mansions, maybe even a celestial choir loft or two, but nothing that really captured my imagination as a place that I'd actually like to live. I'm sure that the language of man can't adequately describe it though, and when I exhale my final breath on Earth, I'll be swept up to Heaven, and will meet God face to face. After a long, comforting embrace, I'm sure that He will step aside and say, "Come look at what I've prepared for you!" I'll probably stand there totally speechless, and after a long period of silence, finally say, "Well, well, well... what do you know about that."

Granddad didn't fear death; in fact, I know that he was keeping a mental list of things that he was going to inquire about when he got to Heaven. For example, in one sermon he was reading about the time in Jesus' life described in John chapter 8, where Jesus was teaching at the temple, and the Pharisees brought a woman to him who had been accused of adultery. They tried to trap Him between his teachings of forgiveness, and Moses' law of severe penalty. Instead of falling for their ruse, the Lord merely knelt down and started writing something in the sand with his finger, until one by one the Pharisees walked away, leaving the woman with no accusers. Jesus said, "Woman, where are those who accuse you? Has no man condemned you?" The woman answered, "No man, Lord." Jesus then said "Then neither do I condemn thee: go, and sin no more." When my grandfather looked up from the Bible, he added, "You know, I've always wondered what our Lord was writing in the sand. I've always felt like it was probably things about each of the Pharisees' lives that were far worse than the sin committed by the woman. I can't be sure, though... but one day I will be. On the day that I meet the Lord in person, that's one of the first questions that I'm going to ask him. In fact, I have a bunch of them that I'm saving up." On the day of his funeral, someone from the family joked that many people on Earth probably didn't get a response to their prayers the day that Granddad died, because all of Heaven was jumping trying to answer a lifetime of curiosities and questions that he'd stored up.

I am human, and I'm not quite at ease with the prospect of my own death. I love my family and friends, my home, and well, my life; the prospect of losing all that and entering a place that I've never seen before, and going through the transition of death, sometimes terrifies me. When that happens, though, I think back to the words of my friend: "Imagine the most perfect day of your life so far – the one day that you'll always remember as the best time you've ever had. Well, heaven's going to be a whole lot better than that." As wonderful as life may seem now, it doesn't hold a candle to what God has in store for us in Heaven. The best news is that you'll never, ever have to leave that magnificent place – you'll get to dwell in the house of the Lord forever.

Chapter 14: But That's Just The Beginning...

Thus ends the 23rd Psalm, but it begins your future. I am certain that if you follow Granddad's advice, contemplating and meditating on the 23rd Psalm, your life will change drastically.

Mine has, and occasionally I'm reminded just how much. I started this book with a story from a year ago when I thought that a business deal gone bad was going to ruin my life. I remember being in the depths of dark depression over the whole incident, and God's power – as described in the words of the 23rd Psalm – pulled me out of it.

For the last year things have continued to build and grow for me, and I hope that this book reflects that wonderful journey and the blessings that I've been given. But just as I was finishing the book and it was time to write this last chapter, something very interesting happened to that same company in which I am a partner. The distributor for our products stopped sending us our monthly payment, and the explanation that they gave didn't make any sense... we knew that something was wrong. On the day that I'm writing this, our distributor padlocked his door, declared bankruptcy, and effectively told all their clients that their money was gone – including ours. In that single moment, we lost thousands of dollars and our distribution channel into stores. I was reminded of last year's catastrophe, which was very, very similar.

There was a major difference, though.

Instead of being distraught and despondent, today I was bopping around, smiling, and thinking about the fact that lightening *never* strikes the same place twice – but it happened to my company. It was almost amusing! The difference was that I now know that the Lord is my shepherd, and I shall not want. Even as a Christian before, I didn't understand the perfect relationship that God wanted to have with me. Now I can see that this may be one of the times when He's making me lie down, but somewhere around me are green pastures. I'm refusing to let myself get bogged down in worry and self-pity. A table is being set for me, and I am confident that my cup will very soon be overflowing.

That's the kind of power that God can instill in you through the words of the 23rd Psalm – that's what He has done for me, and the same thing, and even more, is waiting for you.

That said, I am obligated to end this book with a warning: if you claim the promises made to you by God in the 23rd Psalm, powerful things are going to happen in your life. *Powerful things.* These aren't "iffy" propositions – go back and read what the Psalmist says: I *shall* not want... He *makes* me lie down... He *leads* me... He *restores* my soul... I *will fear* no evil... He *anoints* my head... I *shall* dwell in the house of the Lord forever... all those are absolute, definitive declarations of what is going to happen to you. Not what might occur, not what can possibly come to pass under some circumstances, but what *will* happen if you call upon the Lord to bless you with the words of the 23rd Psalm.

But there are many other aspects to this Psalm. With your blessings come an anointing, and a pressing into service. There is the responsibility that He will make you lie down in green pastures, which may greatly affect your current world. A job may be lost to make way for something greater, or your health may go through a rough spot because God has a plan that requires it... although the pastures will be green in which He places you.

If you claim the words of the 23rd Psalm, you will change. Worry and doubt will be replaced with confidence, want will be replaced with bounty, and fear will be replaced with bravery to face whatever confronts you.

But you will come to see things differently. Your world

that you see in a nice, neat little box may expand to dimensions that you never even imagined.

My Granddad gave the advice that I quoted at the first of this book: "Read and meditate on the 23rd Psalm. Not just one day, but many days. It will change your life; it will make you a different person."

It's not enough to memorize the 23rd Psalm and mindlessly recite it occasionally. Dwell on each verse, then contemplate their meaning and power, and how they relate to you. Spend time with the Psalm every day, but not mechanically or as an afterthought; say it aloud, claiming the power of each verse in your life.

If you're driving to work, thump the steering wheel to accentuate each word of "I shall not want!" Raise your hands high to heaven and claim those words. Don't hesitate to call out your needs: "Lord, my husband is going on a new job interview today, and we need him to do well – we *want* him to succeed. Please bless him!"

Feel free to add your own personal appeal to God: "He leads me in the paths of righteousness for His name sake… and Lord, help me with my job today, because I have hostile customers coming into town for a meeting, and I could use extra blessings!"

Or "Yeah, though I walk through the valley of the shadow… but Lord, today I have to get my test results back from the doctor, and I'm terrified – please help me get through this valley. I need your special blessings today!"

Just don't forget that God leads us in the path of righteousness for His name's sake. While we're looking for all these other blessings promised by the Psalm, we can't ignore the path of doing what's right that He's laid out before us, and we can't dismiss the anointment to serve others with our blessings.

It is so easy to mindlessly recite the 23rd Psalm for a while, and then eventually say, "Well, nothing happened!" On the other hand, if you study, contemplate, and meditate on each verse, claiming their promises and striving to live up to their obligations, your life will change radically and you will experience boundless joy and prosperity for it. Mine has, and I know that yours will as well. It all begins with the blessings that God has for you in 23rd Psalm... *The Lord is my shepherd; I shall not want!*

Share "23"

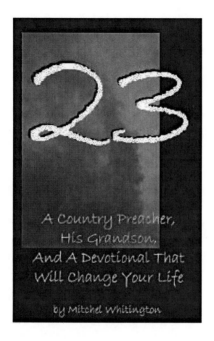

Thank you for taking this journey through the 23rd Psalm with my Granddad and me; I hope that your life will be changed from the experience, as mine has been.

If you've enjoyed "23" and found it to be meaningful in your life, it is easy to share with your friends and family.

"23" is available in bookstores, online at amazon.com, or visit the publisher's site for a copy that is signed by the author:

www.23thebook.com

Thanks again, and may God richly bless your life!

CPSIA information can be obtained
at www.ICGtesting.com
Printed in the USA
LVOW10s1345281016

510684LV00005B/19/P